# Spelling
## Skills

## Grade 1

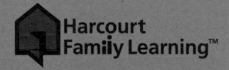

**Harcourt Family Learning™**

© 2005 by Flash Kids
Adapted from *Steck-Vaughn Spelling: Linking Words to Meaning, Level 1*
© 2002 by Harcourt Achieve
Licensed under special arrangement with Harcourt Achieve.

ISBN: 978-1-4114-0382-6

Please submit all inquiries to FlashKids@bn.com

Manufactured in China

Lot #:
31  30
06/17

**Flash Kids**
A Division of Barnes & Noble
122 Fifth Avenue
New York, NY 10011

# Dear Parent,

As your child learns to read and write, he or she is bound to discover that the English language contains very many words, and that no single set of rules is used to spell all of these words. This can feel rather confusing and overwhelming for a young reader. But by completing the fun, straightforward activities in this workbook, your child will build a good foundation for learning spelling skills. To make the path to proper spelling even easier, the first two units focus solely on presenting the alphabet and vowel sounds. Your child will need an understanding of these letters and sounds before he or she can move on to the more difficult activities.

Each of the lessons in units 3 to 6 begin by providing words for your child to say aloud, then write. Next, he or she will complete sentences by filling in missing words. These exercises help him or her to make the connection between a word's appearance and what it sounds like. Your child will then encounter a variety of activities that will strengthen his or her understanding of the meaning and use of each word. These include learning to alphabetize words, using a dictionary, and writing sentences with spelling words. Be sure to have a children's or adult dictionary available for your child to use for some of the exercises. Each lesson also features a short passage containing spelling and grammar mistakes that your child will proofread and correct. Once he or she can recognize both correct and incorrect spellings, your child is ready for the next lesson!

Throughout this workbook are brief unit reviews to help reinforce knowledge of the words that have been learned in the lessons. Your child can use the answer key to check his or her work in the lessons and reviews. Also, take advantage of everyday opportunities to improve spelling skills. By asking your child to spell out words you see inside and outside the home, you are showing your child how often he or she will encounter these words. You can also give your child extra practice in writing these correct spellings by having him or her write a shopping list or note to a family member.

Since learning to spell can be frustrating, your child may wish to use one or more of the spelling strategies on page 6 when he or she finds a word or group of words difficult to master. You can also encourage your child to use the following study steps to learn a word:

1. Say the word. What sounds do you hear?

2. Look at the letters in the word. Think about how each sound is spelled. Close your eyes. Picture the word in your mind.

3. Spell the word aloud.

4. Write the word. Say each letter as you write it.

5. Check the spelling. If you did not spell the word correctly, use the study steps again.

With help from you and this workbook, your child is well on the way to excellent skills in spelling, reading, and writing!

# table of contents

# spelling strategies

What can you do when you aren't sure how to spell a word?

Say the word aloud. Make sure you say it correctly. Listen to the sounds in the word. Think about letters for the sounds.

Guess the spelling of the word and check it in a dictionary.

Write the word in different ways. Choose the spelling that looks correct.

rad   rid   (red)

Draw the shape of the word to help you remember its spelling.

c o l d

Choose a rhyming helper and use it. A rhyming helper is a word that rhymes with the word and is spelled like it.

cat—mat

Create a memory clue to help you remember the spelling.

The tree is by the street.

# STUDY STEPS TO LEARN A WORD

Use the steps on this page to study words that are hard for you.

**1** **Say** the word.
What sounds do you hear?

**2** **Look** at the letters in the word.
Think about how each sound is spelled.
Close your eyes.
Picture the word in your mind.

**3** **Spell** the word aloud.

**4** **Write** the word.
Say each letter as you write it.

**5** **Check** the spelling.
If you did not spell the word correctly,
use the study steps again.

# m, d, f, g

Mouse begins with the m sound.
Write m if the picture name begins
with the m sound.

**mouse**

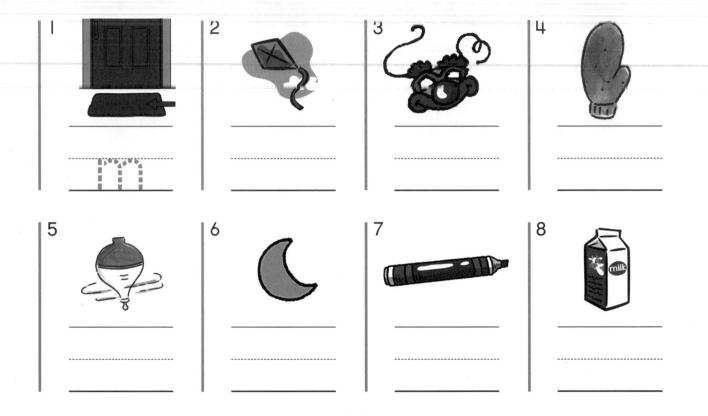

| | | | |
|---|---|---|---|
| 1 | 2 | 3 | 4 |
| 5 | 6 | 7 | 8 |

Possum ends with the m sound. Write m if
the picture name ends with the m sound.

**possum**

| | | | |
|---|---|---|---|
| 9 | 10 | 11 | 12 |

Dog begins with the d sound.
Write d if the picture name
begins with the d sound.

**dog**

| 1 | 2 | 3 | 4 |
|---|---|---|---|
| d ad | uck | ig | oll |

| 5 | 6 | 7 | 8 |
|---|---|---|---|
| esk | oor | ig | un |

Bed ends with the d sound. Write d if the
picture name ends with the d sound.

**bed**

| 9 | 10 | 11 | 12 |
|---|---|---|---|
| li | sa | ca | foo |

Fan begins with the f sound.
Write f if the picture name
begins with the f sound.

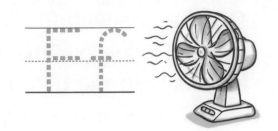

**fan**

| 1 | 2 | 3 | 4 |
|---|---|---|---|
|  | | | |
| f | | | |

| 5 | 6 | 7 | 8 |
|---|---|---|---|

Leaf ends with the f sound. Write f if the
picture name ends with the f sound.

 **leaf**

| 9 | 10 | 11 | 12 |
|---|---|---|---|

Gum begins with the g sound.
Write g if the picture name
begins with the g sound.

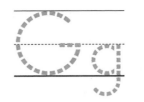  **gum**

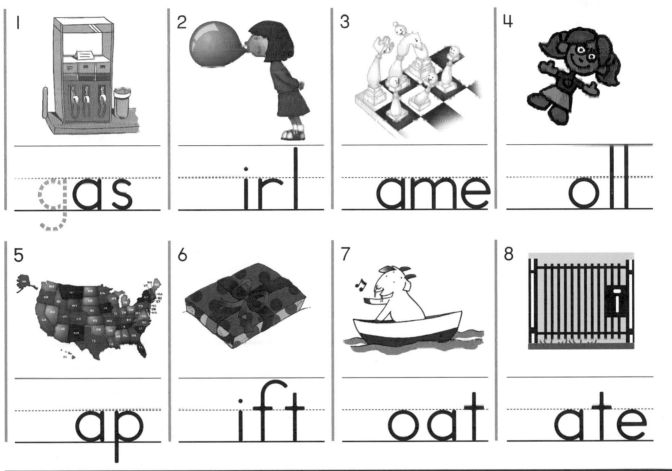

1. g as
2. irl
3. ame
4. oll
5. ap
6. ift
7. oat
8. ate

Log ends with the g sound. Write g if the
picture name ends with the g sound.

**log**

9. pi
10. do
11. ja
12. bu

# b, t, s, w

Bell begins with the b sound.
Write b if the picture name begins
with the b sound.

**bell**

| 1 | 2 | 3 | 4 |
|---|---|---|---|
| b | | | |

| 5 | 6 | 7 | 8 |
|---|---|---|---|

Tub ends with the b sound. Write b if the
picture name ends with the b sound.

**tub**

| 9 | 10 | 11 | 12 |
|---|----|----|----|

Ten begins with the t sound.
Write t if the picture name
begins with the t sound.

**ten**

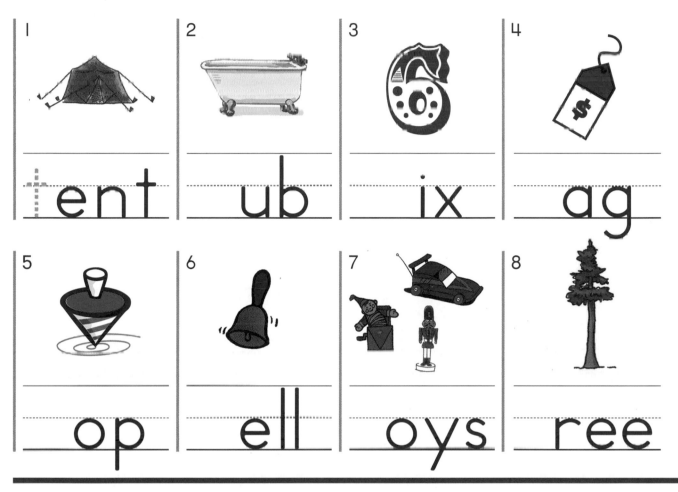

| 1 | 2 | 3 | 4 |
|---|---|---|---|
| tent | ub | ix | ag |
| 5 | 6 | 7 | 8 |
| op | ell | oys | ree |

Net ends with the t sound. Write t if the
picture name ends with the t sound.

**net**

| 9 | 10 | 11 | 12 |
|---|---|---|---|
| ra | nu | do | ba |

Sun begins with the s sound.
Write s if the picture name
begins with the s sound.

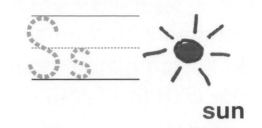

**sun**

| 1 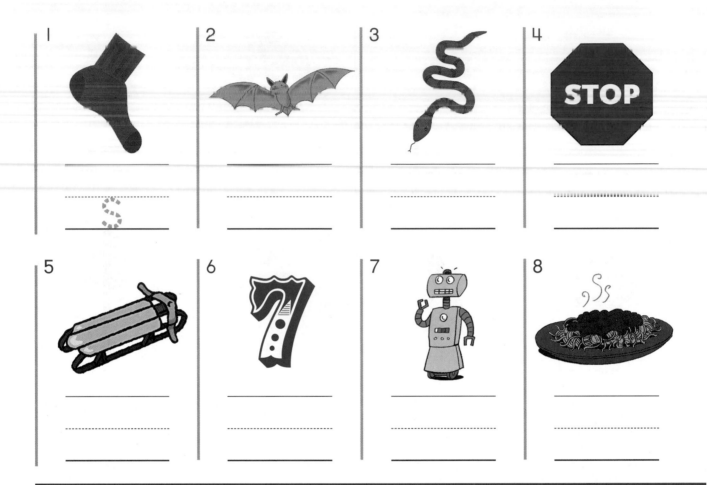 | 2 | 3 | 4 |
|---|---|---|---|
| s | | | |

| 5 | 6 | 7 | 8 |
|---|---|---|---|
| | | | |

Bus ends with the s sound. Write s if the
picture name ends with the s sound.

**bus**

| 9 | 10 | 11 | 12 |
|---|---|---|---|
| | | | |

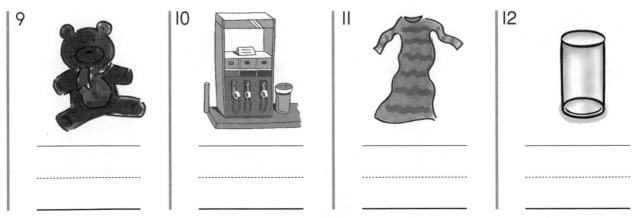

Wig begins with the w sound.
Write w if the picture name
begins with the w sound.

**wig**

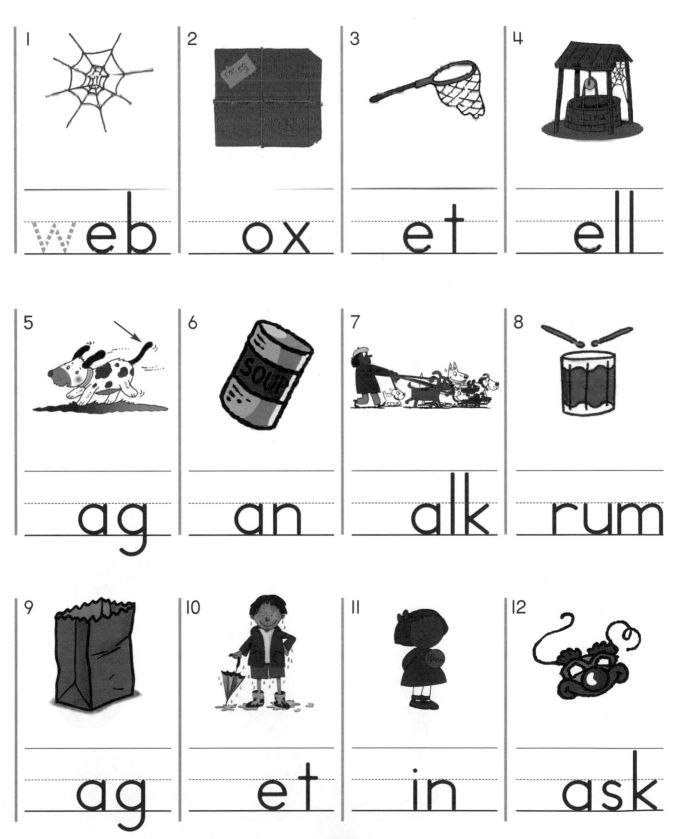

1. w e b

2. _ o x

3. _ e t

4. _ e l l

5. _ a g

6. _ a n

7. _ a l k

8. _ r u m

9. _ a g

10. _ e t

11. _ i n

12. _ a s k

# k, j, p, n

Key begins with the k sound.
Write k if the picture name begins
with the k sound.

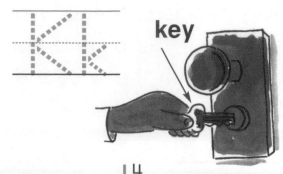

**key**

1

k

2

3

4

5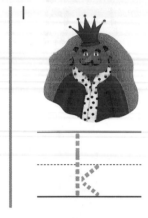

6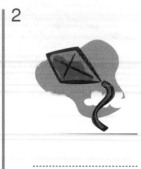

7

8

Book ends with the k sound. Write k if the
picture name ends with the k sound.

**book**

9

10

11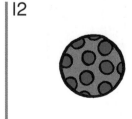

12

Jam begins with the j sound.
Write j if the picture name
begins with the j sound.

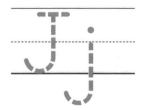 **jam**

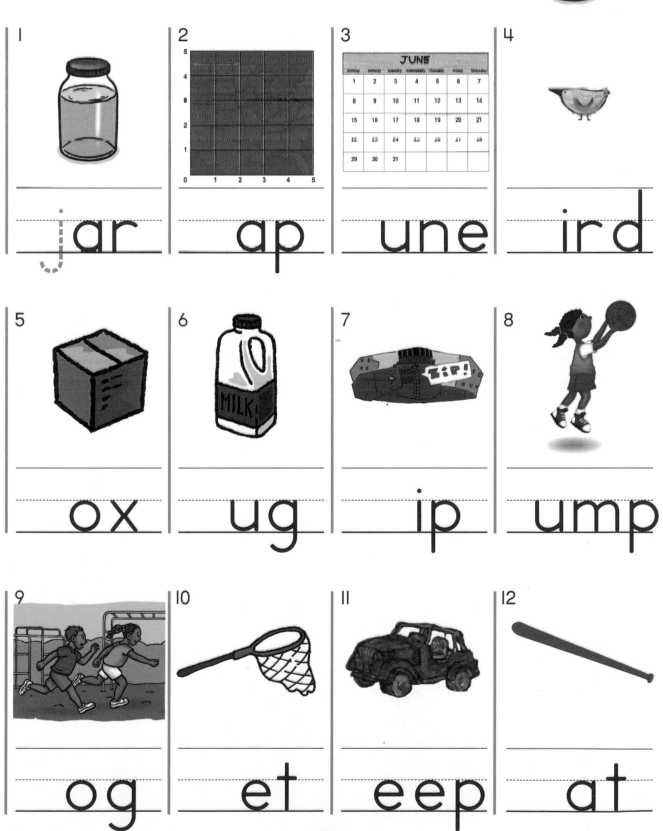

| | | | |
|---|---|---|---|
| 1 | 2 | 3 | 4 |
| j ar | ap | une | ird |
| 5 | 6 | 7 | 8 |
| ox | ug | ip | ump |
| 9 | 10 | 11 | 12 |
| og | et | eep | at |

Pan begins with the p sound.
Write p if the picture name
begins with the p sound.

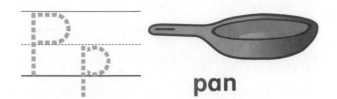

**pan**

| 1 | 2 | 3 | 4 |
|---|---|---|---|
| | | | |

p

| 5 | 6 | 7 | 8 |
|---|---|---|---|
| | | | |

---

Cup ends with the p sound. Write p if the
picture name ends with the p sound.

 **cup**

| 9 | 10 | 11 | 12 |
|---|---|---|---|
| | | | |

Nut begins with the n sound.
Write n if the picture name
begins with the n sound.

**nut**

| 1 | 2 | 3 | 4 |
|---|---|---|---|

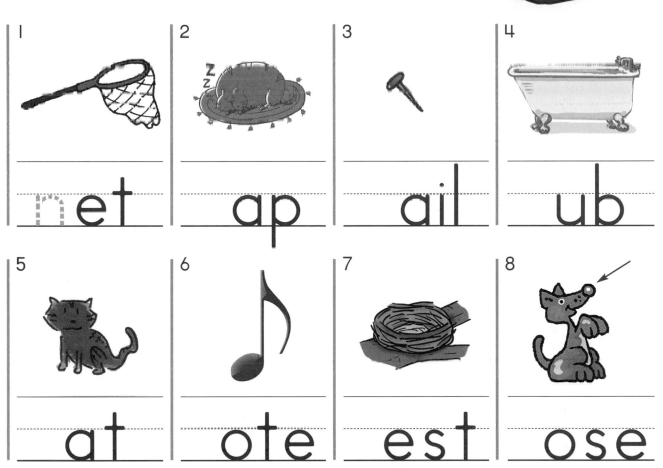

net   ap   ail   ub

| 5 | 6 | 7 | 8 |
|---|---|---|---|

at   ote   est   ose

Can ends with the n sound. Write n if the
picture name ends with the n sound.

**can**

| 9 | 10 | 11 | 12 |
|---|---|---|---|

fa   ru   su   ca

# c, h, l, r

Cat begins with the c sound.
Write c if the picture name begins
with the c sound.

cat

| | | | |
|---|---|---|---|
| 1 | 2 | 3 | 4 |
| c | | | |

| | | | |
|---|---|---|---|
| 5 | 6 | 7 | 8 |

| | | | |
|---|---|---|---|
| 9 | 10 | 11 | 12 |

Hat begins with the h sound.
Write h if the picture name
begins with the h sound.

**hat**

1. _ome

2. _en

3. _hoe

4. _and

5. _urt

6. _ole

7. _op

8. _ook

9. _it

10. _ill

11. _orn

12. _ish

Lamp begins with the l sound.
Write l if the picture name begins
with the l sound.

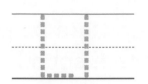

 **lamp**

| 1 | 2 | 3 | 4 |
| 5 | 6 | 7 | 8 |

Snail ends with the l sound. Write l if
the picture name ends with the l sound.

**snail**

| 9 | 10 | 11 | 12 |

Rug begins with the r sound.
Write r if the picture name
begins with the r sound.

**rug**

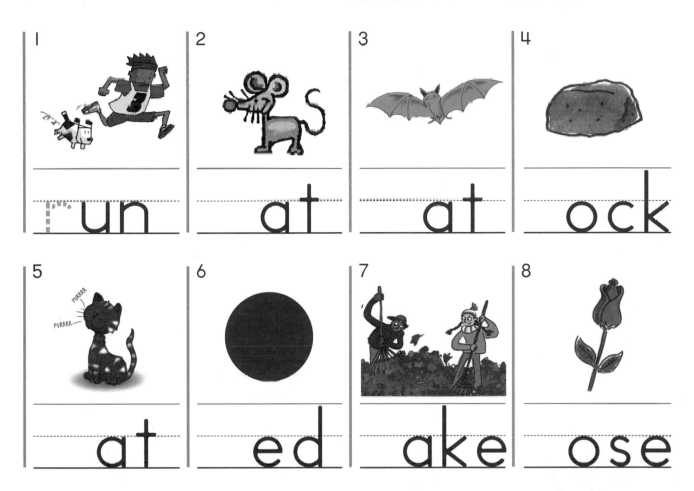

| 1 | 2 | 3 | 4 |
|---|---|---|---|
| r un | at | at | ock |

| 5 | 6 | 7 | 8 |
|---|---|---|---|
| at | ed | ake | ose |

Car ends with the r sound. Write r if the
picture name ends with the r sound.

**car**

| 9 | 10 | 11 | 12 |
|---|---|---|---|
| ja | dru | sta | fou |

# v, y, z, qu, x

Vest begins with the v sound.
Write v if the picture name begins
with the v sound.

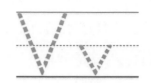

**vest**

| 1 | 2 | 3 | 4 |
|---|---|---|---|
| | | | |

| 5 | 6 | 7 | 8 |
|---|---|---|---|
| | | | |

| 9 | 10 | 11 | 12 |
|---|---|---|---|
| | | | |

Yam begins with the y sound.
Write y if the picture name
begins with the y sound.

Y y

**yam**

| | | | |
|---|---|---|---|
| 1 | 2 | 3 | 4 |
| yo-yo | __at | __arn | __alt |
| 5 | 6 | 7 | 8 |
| __ard | __ag | __olk | __ig |
| 9 | 10 | 11 | 12 |
| __og | __awn | __ift | __ellow |

Zip begins with the z sound. Write
z if the picture name
begins with the z sound.

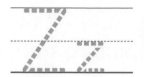

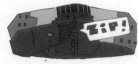

**zip**

| 1 | 2 | 3 | 4 |
|---|---|---|---|
| ZOO | | | |

z

| 5 | 6 | 7 | 8 |
|---|---|---|---|
| | | | Flash Kids 120 Fifth Ave. New York, NY 10011 |

| 9 | 10 | 11 | 12 |
|---|---|---|---|

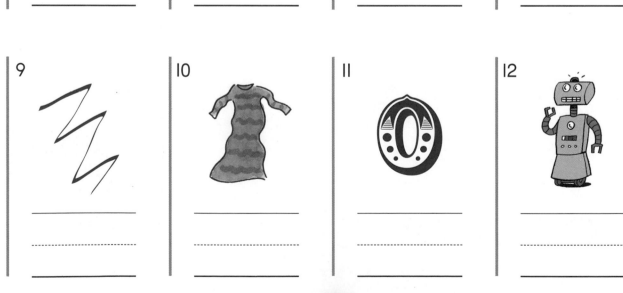

Quilt begins with the qu sound.
Write qu if the picture name
begins with the qu sound.

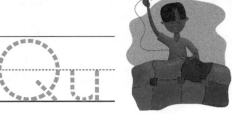

**quilt**

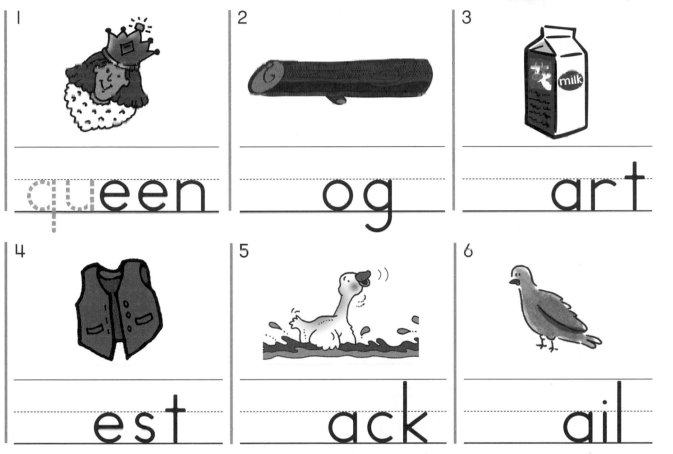

1     queen

2     ___og

3     ___art

4     ___est

5     ___ack

6     ___ail

Six ends with the x sound. Write x if
the picture name ends with the x sound.

**six**

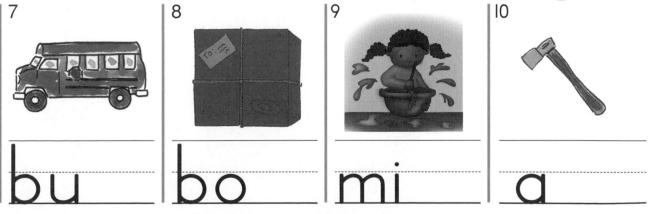

7     bu___

8     bo___

9     mi___

10     a___

# unit 1 Review
## Lessons 1-5

Write the letter that stands for the first sound in each picture name.

m   d   f   g   b   t   s   w   k   j

1

2

3

4

5

6

7

8

9

10

11

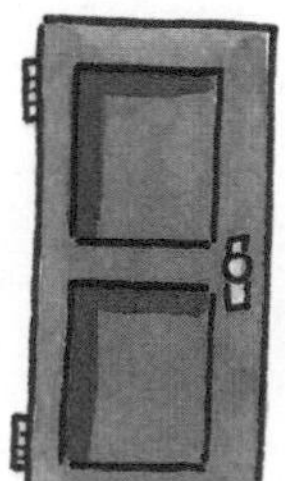

12

# Write the missing letter or letters to complete each word.

m  d  h  s  w  qu  t  n
v  g  p  r  x  y  z  c

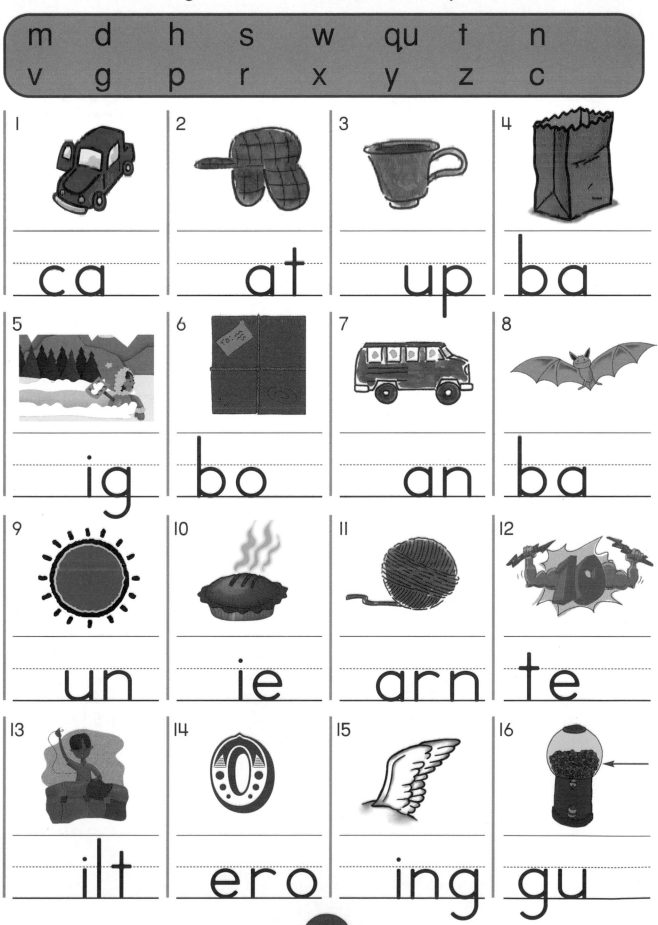

1. ca___

2. ___at

3. ___up

4. ba___

5. ___ig

6. bo___

7. ___an

8. ba___

9. ___un

10. ___ie

11. ___arn

12. ___te

13. ___ilt

14. ___ero

15. ___ing

16. gu___

# Short a

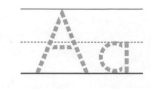

cat

Cat has the short a sound.
Say each picture name.
Write a if you hear the short a sound.

1

_____

a

2

_____

3

_____

4

_____

5

_____

6

_____

7

_____

8

_____

9

_____

10

_____

11

SOUP

_____

12

$

_____

Say each picture name.
Write a if you hear the short a sound.
Color each short a picture.

1
h a m

2
p n

3
c p

4
m p

5
b x

6
b g

7
p g

8
h t

9
m t

Say the word that names the first picture.
Circle the pictures whose names rhyme with the word.

1 pan

2 bag

3 cat

4 cap

5 sad

Say each picture name. Trace the first letter.
Then write an to make the word.

| 1 | 2 | 3 |
|---|---|---|
| f | v | p |

| 4 | 5 | 6 |
|---|---|---|
| m | c | t |

Say each picture name. Trace the first letter.
Then write at to make the word.

| 7 | 8 | 9 |
|---|---|---|
| b | c | h |

| 10 | 11 |
|---|---|
| m | r |

# Short e

Bed has the short e sound.
Say each picture name.
Write e if you hear the short e sound.

E e    **bed**

1

_____
- - - - - - -
_____

2

_____
- - - - - - -
_____

3

_____
- - - - - - -
_____

4

_____
- - - - - - -
_____

5

_____
- - - - - - -
_____

6

_____
- - - - - - -
_____

7

_____
- - - - - - -
_____

8

_____
- - - - - - -
_____

9

_____
- - - - - - -
_____

10

_____
- - - - - - -
_____

11

_____
- - - - - - -
_____

12

_____
- - - - - - -
_____

Say each picture name.
Write e if you hear the short e sound.
Color each short e picture.

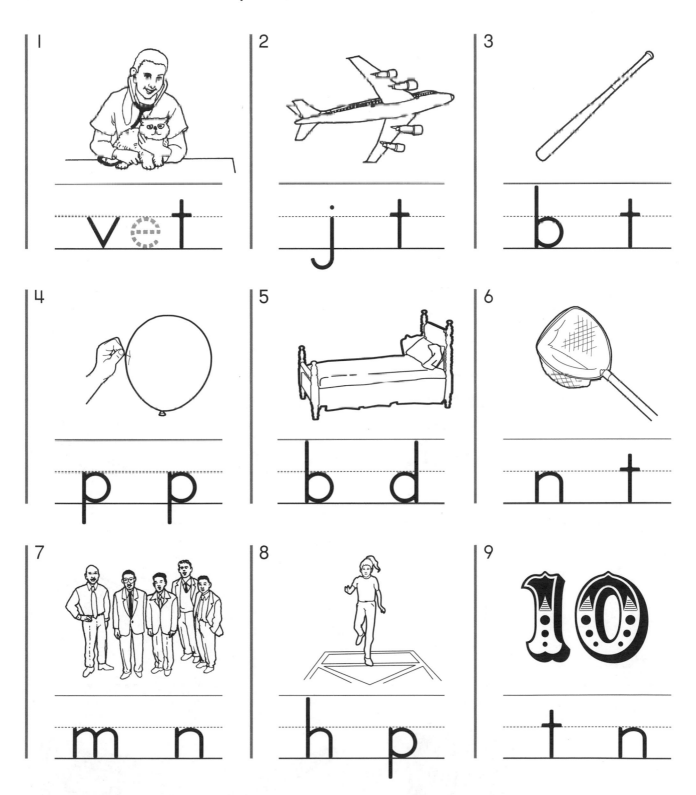

1. v e t

2. j _ t

3. b _ t

4. p _ p

5. b _ d

6. n _ t

7. m _ n

8. h _ p

9. t _ n

Say the word that names the first picture.
Circle the pictures whose names rhyme with the word.

1  bed

2  bell

3  leg

4  vet

5  hen

Say each picture name. Trace the first letter or letters.
Then write ell to make the word.

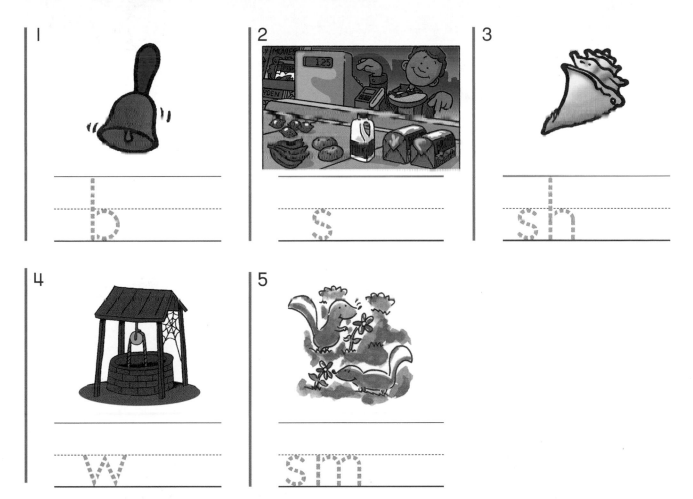

1. b____
2. s____
3. sh____
4. w____
5. sm____

Say each picture name. Trace the first letter.
Then write en to make the word.

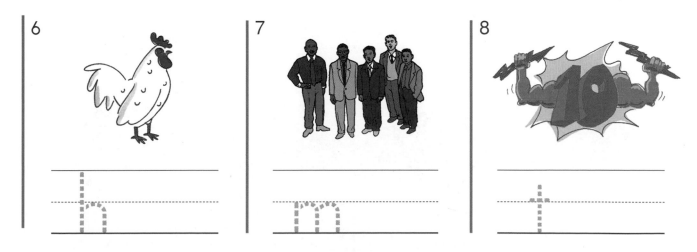

6. h____
7. m____
8. t____

# Short i

Pig has the short i sound.
Say each picture name.
Write i if you hear the short i sound.

**pig**

| 1 | 2 | 3 | 4 |
|---|---|---|---|
| | | | |
| i | | | |

| 5 | 6 | 7 | 8 |
|---|---|---|---|

| 9 | 10 | 11 | 12 |
|---|---|---|---|

Say each picture name.
Write i if you hear the short i sound.
Color each short i picture.

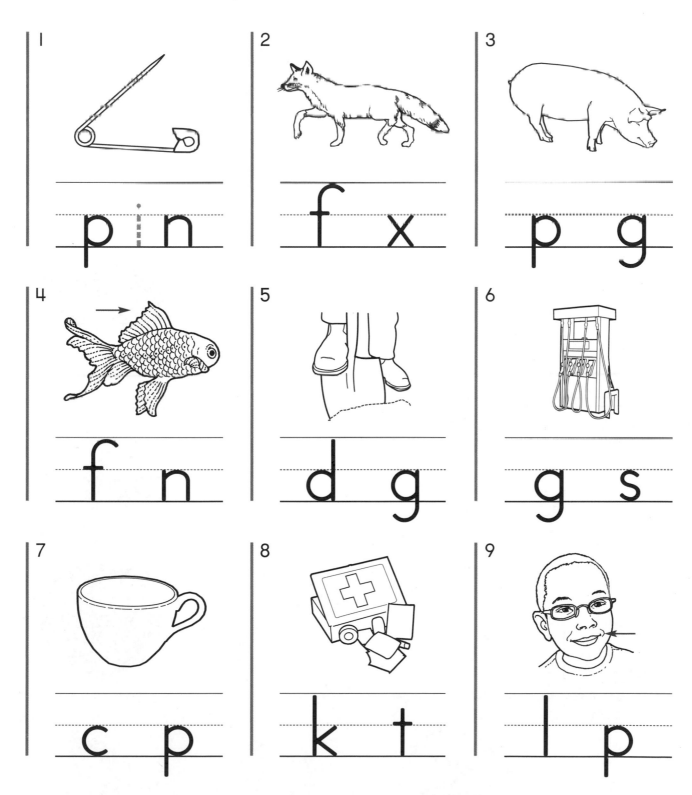

1. p i n

2. f __ x

3. p __ g

4. f __ n

5. d __ g

6. g __ s

7. c __ p

8. k __ t

9. l __ p

Say the word that names the first picture.
Circle the pictures whose names rhyme with the word.

1 | pin

2 | kit

3 | lip

4 | pig

5 | fix

Say each picture name. Trace the first letter.
Then write it to make the word.

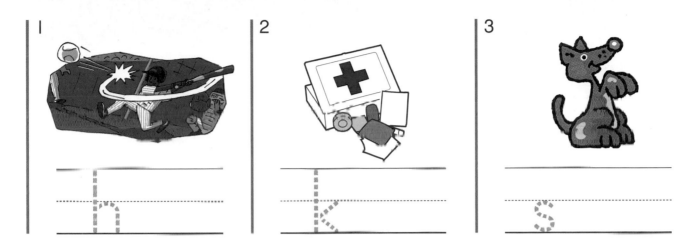

| 1 | 2 | 3 |
| --- | --- | --- |
| b | k | s |

Say each picture name. Trace the first letter.
Then write ig to make the word.

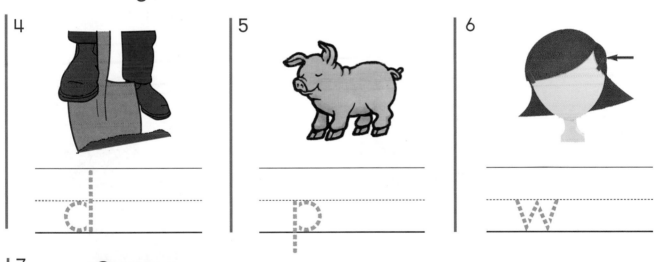

| 4 | 5 | 6 |
| --- | --- | --- |
| d | p | w |

7

b

# Short o

Pop has the short o sound.
Say each picture name.
Write o if you hear the short o sound.

**pop**

Say each picture name.
Write o if you hear the short o sound.
Color each short o picture.

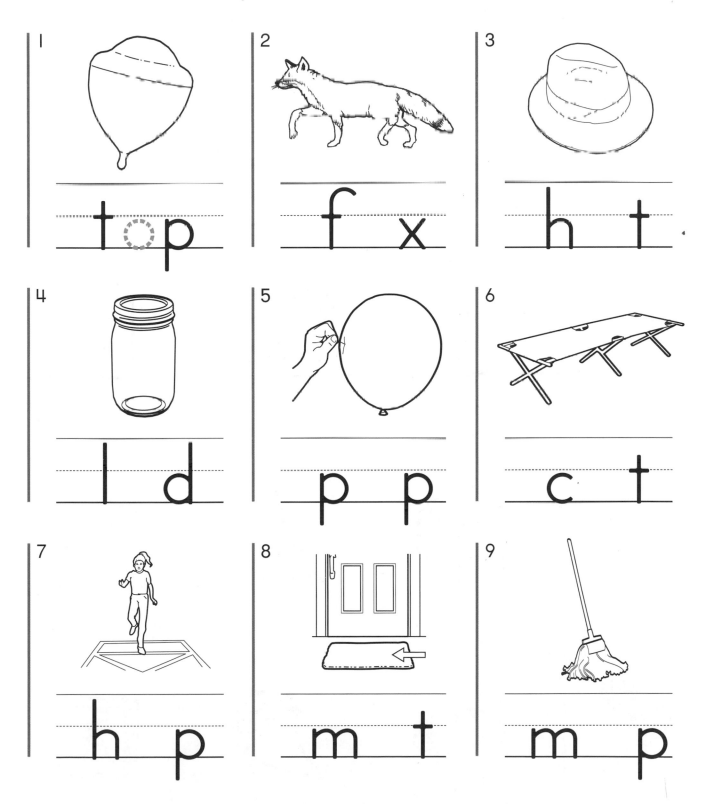

1. t o p

2. f _ x

3. h _ t

4. l _ d

5. p _ p

6. c _ t

7. h _ p

8. m _ t

9. m _ p

Say the word that names the first picture.
Circle the pictures whose names rhyme with the word.

1
hot

2
fox

3
pop

4
sock

Say each picture name. Trace the first letter.
Then write op to make the word.

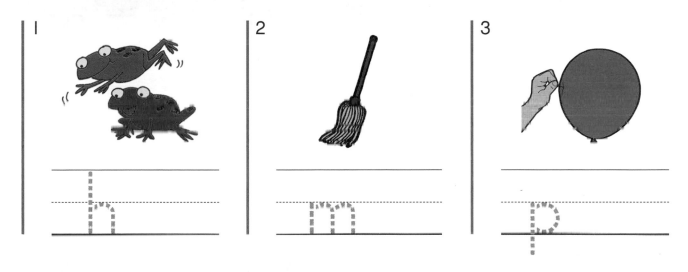

1  h

2  m

3  p

Say each picture name. Trace the first letter or letters.
Then write ot to make the word.

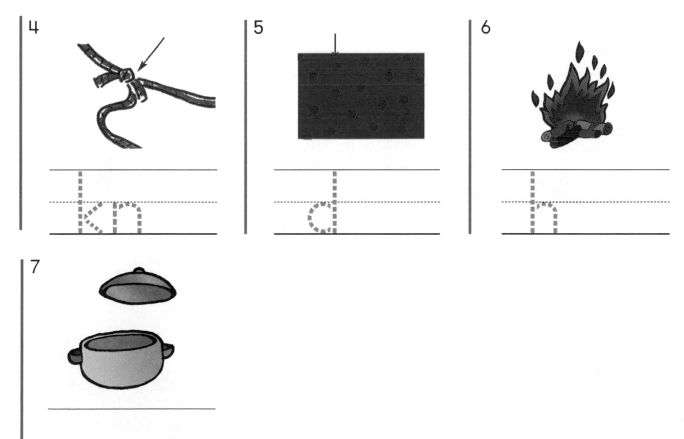

4  kn

5  d

6  h

7  p

# Short u

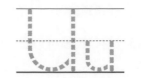

**cup**

Cup has the short u sound.
Say each picture name.
Write u if you hear the short u sound.

| 1 | 2 | 3 | 4 |
|---|---|---|---|
| | | | |
| u | | | |

| 5 | 6 | 7 | 8 |
|---|---|---|---|
| | | | |

| 9 | 10 | 11 | 12 |
|---|---|---|---|
| | | | |

Say each picture name.
Write u if you hear the short u sound.
Color each short u picture.

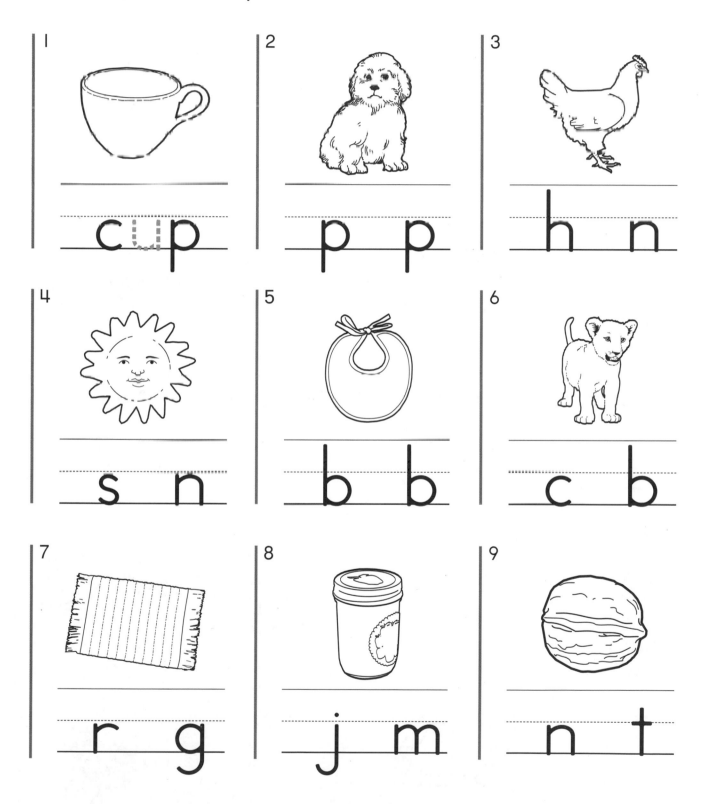

1 c u p

2 p ___ p

3 h ___ n

4 s ___ n

5 b ___ b

6 c ___ b

7 r ___ g

8 j ___ m

9 n ___ t

Say the word that names the first picture.
Circle the pictures whose names rhyme with the word.

1  hut

2  sun

3  tub

4  gum

5  mug

Say each picture name.
Trace the first letter.
Then write ug to make the word.

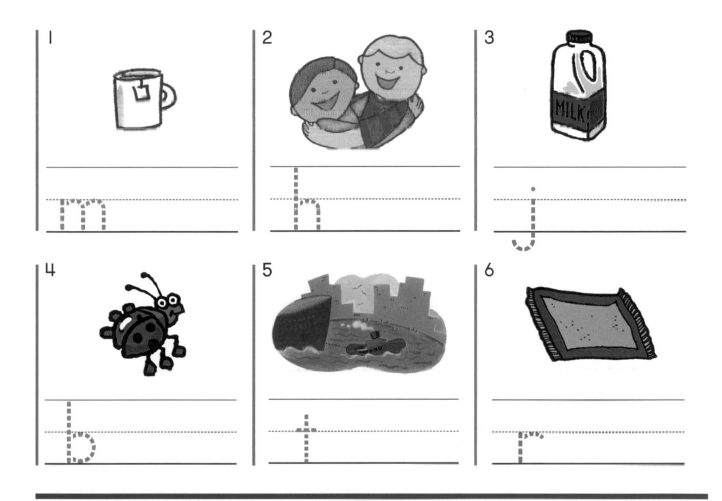

1  m

2  h

3  j

4  b

5  t

6  r

Say each picture name. Trace the first letter.
Then write ut to make the word.

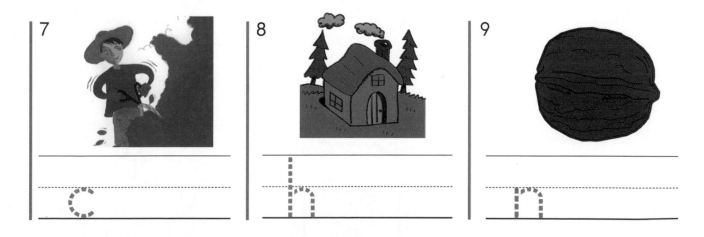

7  c

8  h

9  n

# unit 2 Review
## LESSONS 6-10

Say each picture name. Circle the letter for the vowel sound. Then write the letter.

cat      bed      pig      pop      cup

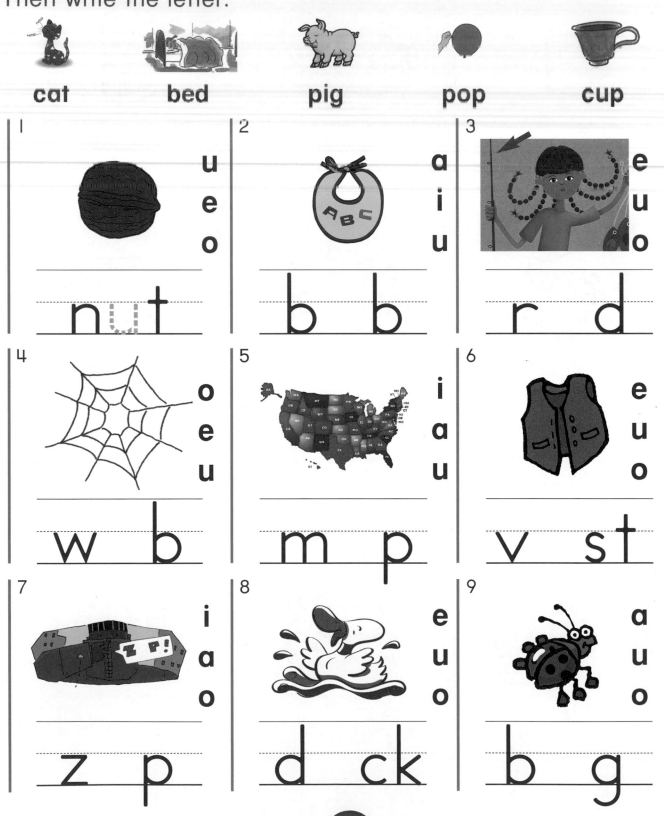

1. u e o    n u t

2. a i u    b b

3. e u o    r d

4. o e u    w b

5. i a u    m p

6. e u o    v st

7. i a o    z p

8. e u o    d ck

9. a u o    b g

Say each picture name. Trace the first letter.
Then write the letters from the box that complete the name.

an     en     in     op     ut

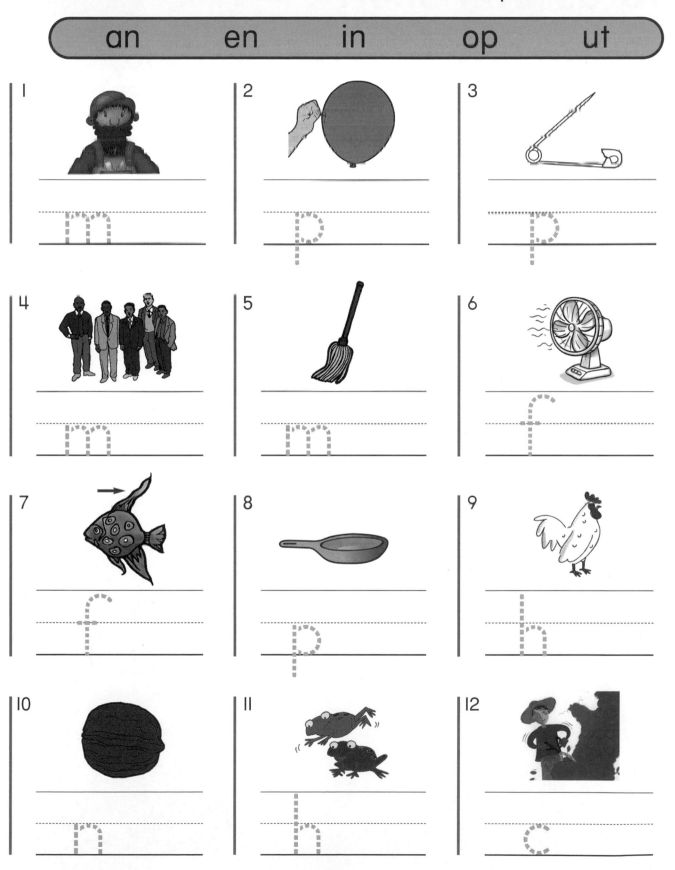

1   m

2   p

3   p

4   m

5   m

6   f

7   f

8   p

9   h

10   n

11   h

12   c

# Words with Short a

**Say and Write**

1. am

2. at

3. can

4. ran

5. fast

6. last

The short a sound can be spelled a, like ran and fast.

## Spell and Write

Write the spelling word that completes each sentence.

1.   I _____ Pam.

2.   A duck _____ swim.

3.   The dog is _____ the park.

4.   The pig _____ to him.

5.   My dog can run _____ .

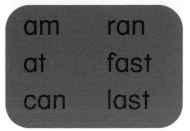

6.   The frog is _____ .

# Read and Write

Write the spelling words to complete
the story.

am
at
can
ran
fast
last

_____

Randy Rabbit _____ on a path.  The path

_____

was _____ the park.  Randy ran well.  He ran

_____          _____

_____.  That was _____ week.

_____

Now  he will run again.  "I _____ ready," Randy

_____

says.  "I _____ do it!"

## Proofreading

Circle each word that is spelled wrong.
Write the word correctly.

Dad,

Lunch is et 11:00.

We cin meet then.

I im in Room 102.

Sam

1. _____

2. _____

3. _____

## Language Skills

A sentence that tells something ends with a period.

Write each sentence correctly.

**Lad is my dog.**

**4.** Lad is fast

_____

_____

**5.** We ran to Dad

_____

_____

**6.** I was the last one

_____

_____

# More Words with Short a

### Say and Write

1. sat

2. van

3. has

4. hand

5. that

6. have

The short a sound can be spelled a, like van and hand.

# Spell and Write

Write the spelling word that completes each sentence.

1.  Mack has a _____,

2.  Will you get _____ for me?

3.  Dan can draw his _____.

4.  Jan _____ by her pal.

5.  Hal and Jack _____ big bags.

6. My cat _____ a bell.

# Read and Write

Write the spelling words to complete
the selection.

sat
van
has
hand
that
have

_____

Nan _____ with her dad.  They sat in their

_____                    _____

_____ . Nan had a book in her _____.

She got it from the library in her town.  The library

_____

_____ many good books to read.  Nan likes

_____                    _____

_____ library.  Do you _____ a library

where you live?

# Proofreading

Circle each word that is spelled wrong.
Write the word correctly.

> ## Jack's List
>
> 1. Help wash the vaan.
>
> 2. Find out who hes my cap.
>
> 3. Get thut book for Gran.

1. _____

2. _____

3. _____

# Language Skills

A sentence begins with a capital letter.

**Stan has a van.**

Write each sentence correctly.

**4.** we have a van.

_____

_____

**5.** i sat in back.

_____

_____

**6.** mom held my hand.

_____

_____

# Words with Short e

**Say and Write**

1. end

2. ten

3. red

4. wet

5. tell

6. seven

The short e sound can be spelled e, like end and tell.

# Spell and Write

Write the spelling word that completes each sentence.

1.  The dog is _____.

2.  Ben's hat is _____.

3.  Five plus five is _____.

4. 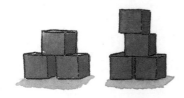 I am at the _____ of the line.

5.  Three plus four is _____.

6.  Mr. Silva will _____ a story.

# Read and Write

Write the spelling words to complete the story.

end
ten
red
wet
tell
seven

Rex washes his socks.  Some are _____.

Some are white.  The socks are dripping _____.

Rex puts them on the line.  He has five pairs.  There are

_____ socks on the line.  Three socks on the

_____ fall.  Now only _____ socks

are on the line.  Who will _____ Rex?

# Proofreading

Circle each word that is spelled wrong.
Write the word correctly.

There were tun pets in bed.

Then sevin fell out.

How does this story ind?

1. _____

2. _____

3. _____

# Dictionary Skills

Look at a dictionary. The words are in ABC order. Words that begin with a come first.

4. Write the first word in your dictionary.

_____

_____

5. Write the last word in your dictionary.

_____

_____

6. Write a dictionary word that begins with c.

_____

_____

7. Write a dictionary word that begins with m.

_____

_____

# More Words with Short e

**Say and Write**

1. get

2. pet

3. help

4. went

5. best

6. when

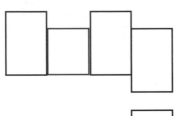

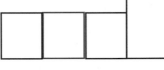

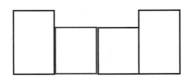

The short e sound can be spelled e, like pet and help.

# Spell and Write

Write the spelling word that completes each sentence.

| get | went |
|-----|------|
| pet | best |
| help | when |

1. Brett's _____ is a dog.

2. My cat naps _____ I nap.

3. This dog is the _____!

4. Dad _____ to the store.

5. Ted and Ned _____ the plants.

6. Ken can _____ his mom.

## Read and Write

Write the spelling words to
complete the selection.

get
pet
help
went
best
when

_____

A puppy is a good _____. Would you like

_____                          _____

to _____ a puppy?  You can _____

_____

take care of it.  You can feed your puppy _____

it is hungry.  You can play with it.  You will wonder where

_____

the time _____.  Do you think a puppy is the

_____

_____ pet?

## Proofreading

Circle each word that is spelled wrong.
Write the word correctly.

Help Wanted

I need help with my pett.

You must feed it whin I am gone.

I need the bist.

1. _____

2. _____

3. _____

## Writing

Write a sentence about a pet. Use a spelling word.

_____

_____

_____

_____

# Words with Short i

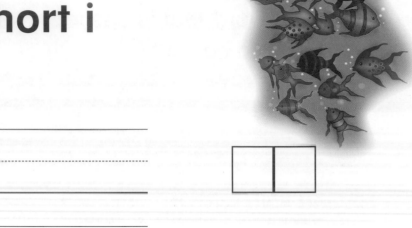

**Say and Write**

1.  in

2.  is

3.  it

4.  with

5.  sick

6.  quit

The short i sound can be spelled i, like in and sick.

## Spell and Write

Write the spelling word that completes each sentence.

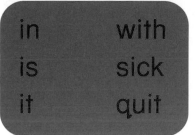

| in | with |
| is | sick |
| it | quit |

1. Nick feels _____.

2. I have milk _____ my fish.

3. He _____ happy.

4. Kim plays _____ the yard.

5. Jim wants the rain to _____.

6. The flower has a bee on _____.

## Read and Write

Write the spelling words to complete
the selection.

in
is
it
with
sick
quit

_____

Sometimes people get _____. Then they

_____          _____

must stay _____ bed.  It _____ not

much fun.  You can make a picture for a sick friend.  Get

_____

some paper.  Draw on _____.  Paint on it

_____          _____

_____ bright colors.  Don't _____ until

it looks great.  Give it to your friend.  Say, "Get well quick!"

# Proofreading

Circle each word that is spelled wrong.
Write the word correctly.

Will,

Are you seok?

Hot tea iz good.

Stay en bed and rest.

Jim

1. _____

2. _____

3. _____

# Dictionary Skills

Write the spelling words in ABC order.

quit     with     it     sick

4. _____

5. _____

6. _____

7. _____

## Word Math

Add letters and take away letters.
Write the spelling word.

am   can   fast

1. ham – h – _____

2. fan – n + st = _____

3. cap – p + n = _____

## Proofreading

Circle the word that is spelled wrong. Write it correctly.

has   that   have

4. Dad and I hav hats. _____

5. The dog haas a hat? _____

6. Is thet my hat? _____

## Missing Words

Write the word that completes each sentence.

**get    help    when**

1. Ben will _____ a puppy.

2. Beth likes to _____ Dad cook.

3. We will go _____ it gets dark.

## What's the Right Word?

The word in dark type does not make sense in the sentence. Write the spelling word that makes sense.

**in    sick    with**

4. Rex is white **quit** brown spots. _____

5. Do you feel **pig**? _____

6. The cans are **it** the bag. _____

# More Words with Short i

**Say and Write**

1. if

2. six

3. sit

4. big

5. did

6. this

The short i sound can be spelled i, like six and big.

# Spell and Write

Write the spelling word that completes each sentence.

1. Milly has _____ puppies.

2. We will get wet _____ it rains.

3. We _____ together.

4. The red box is the _____ one.

5. Dad and I _____ the shopping.

6. I drew _____.

## Read and Write

Write the spelling words to complete the story.

| if |
|:---:|
| six |
| sit |
| big |
| did |
| this |

I have _____ little kittens.  My kittens will

not always be little.  Soon they will be _____.

The kittens _____ on me.  They go to sleep

in my lap.  They wake up _____ I move.  Then

_____ is what they do.  They cry, "Mew! Mew!"

They _____ it just now!

# Proofreading

Circle each word that is spelled wrong.
Write the word correctly.

Sis,

You left a bigg mess!

I diid not like it.

Please pick up thes mess now!

Sid

1. _____

2. _____

3. _____

# Dictionary Skills

Circle the first letter of each word.
Write each group of words in ABC order.

**4.** big   am   can

_____

_____

_____

**5.** six   if   has

_____

_____

_____

**6.** this   sit   ran

_____

_____

_____

# Words with Short o

**Say and Write**

1. on

2. top

3. not

4. hop

5. hot

6. stop

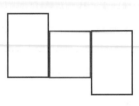
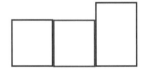

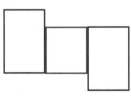

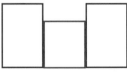

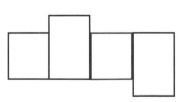

The short o sound can be spelled o, like hop and stop.

# Spell and Write

Write the spelling word that completes each sentence.

| | |
|---|---|
| on | hop |
| top | hot |
| not | stop |

1. A frog can _____.

2. We must _____ and wait.

3. The lamp is _____ the table.

4. Dot is _____.

5. Roxie will _____ come.

6. The little box is on _____.

## Read and Write

Write the spelling words to complete the story.

on
top
not
hop
hot
stop

Bonnie likes to _____. She hops and hops.

Bonnie hops _____ the path. She hops on the

grass. She does _____ fall. Then she hops

to the _____ of the hill. When will Bonnie

_____? She will have to stop when she gets

too _____!

# Proofreading

Circle each word that is spelled wrong.
Write the word correctly.

Rules for Safe Biking

Put your helmet un.

Do nott ride too fast.

Stap at red lights.

1. _____

2. _____

3. _____

# Language Skills

A sentence that asks a question ends with a question mark.

**Where is Mopsy?**

Write each sentence correctly.

**4.** Is Mopsy at the top

_____

_____

**5.** Is Mopsy hot

_____

_____

**6.** Will he hop down

_____

_____

# More Words with Short o

## Say and Write

1. fox

2. mop

3. job

4. box

5. lock

6. sock

The short o sound can be spelled o, like fox and socks.

# Spell and Write

Write the spelling word that completes each sentence.

1.   _____
   Ron lost a _____.

2.   _____
   Dot can _____ up the mess.

3.   _____
   Mom has a _____ at school.

4.   _____
   A _____ lives in the woods.

5.   _____
   Tom put a key in the _____.

6.   _____
   The toys go in a _____.

## Read and Write

Write the spelling words to
complete the story.

fox
mop
job
box
lock
sock

_____

Bob the ox had a _____ to do.  He had to

_____        _____

_____.  A _____ came in.  He had

_____

a _____.  The fox took out a brush.  "Put this

_____

on your _____," he said.

Bob did it.  Then he put a brush on his other sock.

He started to mop.  "This is fast!" Bob said.  "Soon I can

_____

_____ up and go have fun!"

# Proofreading

Circle each word that is spelled wrong.
Write the word correctly.

I have a jub to do.

I put the toys in the bax.

Then Mom can moop my room.

I. _____

2. _____

3. _____

# Writing

Write a sentence about a job you do.
Use a spelling word.

_____

_____

_____

# Words with Short u

**Say and Write**

1. us
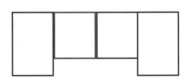

2. run

3. fun
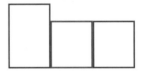

4. jump

5. much

6. duck

The short u sound can be spelled u, like run and duck.

## Spell and Write

Write the spelling word that completes each sentence.

1. Bud walks with _____.

2. They can _____ fast.

3. Meg and Gus _____ rope.

4. She feeds the _____.

5. Josh and Mack had _____.

6. How _____ will Gran read?

# Read and Write

Write the spelling words to complete
the selection.

us
run
fun
jump
much
duck

_____

A baby _____ is called a duckling.  A

_____

duckling cannot _____ fast.  A duckling can have

_____          _____

_____.  It can _____ into the water.

It can swim, too.  The mother duck quacks if a duckling

swims too far away.  She is saying, "You have gone

_____          _____

_____ too far.  Come back to _____!"

## Proofreading

Circle each word that is spelled wrong.
Write the word correctly.

Dusty,

Thanks for coming to see os.

I had fon with you.

I like you very mach.

Sunny

1. _____

2. _____

3. _____

## Writing

Write a sentence about someone you like.
Use a spelling word.

_____

_____

_____

# More Words with Short u

## Say and Write

1. up

2. cut

3. bus

4. but

5. must

6. just

The short u sound can be spelled u, like up and bus.

# Spell and Write

Write the spelling word that completes each sentence.

1. She will ride the _____ .

2. Russ _____ pick up the toys.

3. Sunny will _____ the string.

4. The girls look _____ alike.

5. It is cold, _____ there is no snow.

6. The ball goes _____ and down.

## Read and Write

Write the spelling words to complete
the selection.

up
cut
bus
but
must
just

_____

Do you know what to do on a _____?

_____

You _____ sit down when the bus is moving.

_____

You cannot stand _____. You can play a game.

_____

You can sing a song, too. You can draw, _____

_____

do not use scissors. You might _____ yourself.

_____

You can read, or you can _____ sit and rest.

## Proofreading

Circle each word that is spelled wrong.
Write the word correctly.

I jist saw Chuck.

He was on the bos.

We mest get him on our team.

1. _____

2. _____

3. _____

## Language Skills

Use is to write about one thing.
Use are to write about more than one thing.

Write the sentences. Use is and are correctly.

4. The cut ____ on my hand.

_____

_____

5. My house ____ up the street.

_____

_____

6. We ____ going home now.

_____

_____

# Unit 4 Review
## Lessons 16–20

## Missing Letters

Write the missing letter. Then write the word.

big   did   this

1. d _____ d   _____

2. th _____ s   _____

3. b _____ g   _____

## Proofreading

Circle the word that is spelled wrong.
Write it correctly.

on   not   stop

4. The rain will stap soon.   _____

5. I will play un the sidewalk.   _____

6. I do nat like to stay inside.   _____

# Label the Picture

The words in the box go in this picture.
Write each word on the correct line.

job    box    sock

# Words with Long a

**Say and Write**

1. name

2. game

3. same

4. made

5. make

6. take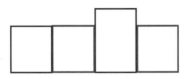

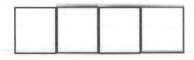
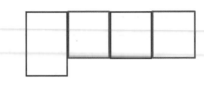

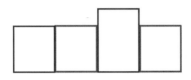
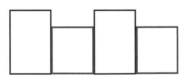

The long a sound can be spelled a_e, like game and take.

# Spell and Write

Write the spelling word that completes each sentence.

1. They will _____ a snack.

2. Jake and Kate play a _____.

3. The cat's _____ is Gabe.

4. Are the socks the _____?

5. Jade will _____ her lunch.

6. Tate _____ a plane.

## Read and Write

Write the spelling words to complete
the selection.

Polly plays the piano with her pet parrot.

name
game
same
made
make
take

_____                     _____

What is your _____? Play a _____

_____

with your name. To begin, _____ the first letter of

your name, such as **P**. Think of words that begin with the

_____                     _____

_____ letter. Next, _____ a sentence

with the words. Then, add more words to the sentence you

_____

_____.

## Proofreading

Circle each word that is spelled wrong.
Write the word correctly.

Mom let me tak a dog home.

I have to give him a naam.

We will play a geme.

1. _____

2. _____

3. _____

## Writing

Write a sentence about a game you like.
Use a spelling word.

_____

_____

_____

# More Words with Long a

## Say and Write

1. day

2. may

3. say

4. pay

5. stay

6. play

The long a sound can be spelled ay, like pay and play.

# Spell and Write

Write the spelling word that completes each sentence.

1. _____
   Jay will _____ for the book.

2. _____
   It is a nice _____.

3. _____
   Fay must _____ in bed.

4. _____
   It _____ rain today.

5. _____
   The kitten likes to _____.

6. _____
   What will Mom _____?

## Read and Write

Write the spelling words to complete the selection.

day

may

say

pay

stay

play

Some work places have a special _____.

Children _____ go to work with an adult.  They

can _____ all day.  They learn about jobs.  They

have fun, but it is not a time to _____.  The

children _____ they learn a lot. They see how

adults work for their _____.

# Proofreading

Circle each word that is spelled wrong.
Write the word correctly.

Wayne,

Will you come stae with me?

We could pla a lot.

Please sey you will.

Jake

1. _____

2. _____

3. _____

# Language Skills

Sentences begin with a capital letter.
Names of people begin with a capital letter, too.

**We play with Jay.**

Write each sentence correctly.

4. we may play with jay all day.

_____

_____

5. he will pay kay today.

_____

_____

# Words with Long e

**Say and Write**

1. me

2. we

3. he

4. be

5. she

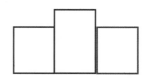

6. eat

The long e sound can be spelled e or ea, like we and eat.

# Spell and Write

Write the spelling word that completes each sentence.

1. _____
   _ _ _ _ _ _ _ _ _ _ _ _ _ _ _ _ _ _ _
   "Are _____ _____ late?" Lee asked.

2. _____
   _ _ _ _ _ _ _ _ _ _ _ _ _ _ _ _ _ _
   It is time to _____.

3. _____
   _ _ _ _ _ _ _ _ _ _ _ _ _ _ _ _ _
   Is _____ calling Mom?

4. _____
   _ _ _ _ _ _ _ _ _ _ _ _ _ _ _ _ _ _
   "Will you help _____?" he asked.

5. _____
   _ _ _ _ _ _ _ _ _ _ _ _ _ _ _ _
   She will _____ awake soon.

6. _____ Will _____ come and play?

## Read and Write

Write the spelling words to complete the story.

me
we
he
be
she
eat

My family sleeps a lot in winter.  We need food before

_____ _____

_____ sleep.  We _____ a lot!

_____

Today Mom showed _____ how to catch fish.

_____

Then _____ showed my brother.  I know

_____

_____ likes fish.  Soon we will find a cave.

_____

A cave is a good place to _____ in winter.

# Proofreading

Circle each word that is spelled wrong.
Write the word correctly.

> Neal,
>
> Can you bea home by 3:00?
>
> Then wi will go to the game.
>
> Dad said hee will take us.
>
> Jean

1. _____

2. _____

3. _____

# Language Skills

Unscramble each sentence and write it.
Use capital letters and periods correctly.

**4.** my went me with sister

_____

_____

**5.** likes be me she to with

_____

_____

**6.** eat to we pizza went

_____

_____

# More Words with Long e

## Say and Write

1. see

2. feet

3. keep

4. tree

5. street

6. three

The long e sound can be spelled ee, like in tree or see.

# Spell and Write

Write the spelling word that completes each sentence.

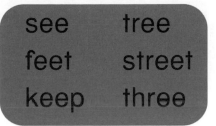

1. A leaf fell from the _____.

2. They walk across the _____.

3. This thing has many _____.

4. What does she _____?

5. Pete can _____ things in the box.

6. The _____ kittens play all day.

## Read and Write

Write the spelling words to complete the story.

see<br>
feet<br>
keep<br>
tree<br>
street<br>
three

Dee's dad took her on a hike with _____ of

her friends.  They all live on the same _____.

"Please _____ walking on the trail," Dad said.

Something went splash!  "What is on the other side of that

_____?" Dad asked.

"I _____ a creek!" Lee said.  "Some kids are

in the water.  May we get our _____ wet, too?"

## Proofreading

Circle each word that is spelled wrong.
Write the word correctly.

We planted a trea.

It will kep growing.

It will be 12 fete tall.

1. _____

2. _____

3. _____

## Dictionary Skills

Look up each word in a dictionary.
Copy the sentence that helps you
know what the word means.

4. see

_____

_____

5. street

_____

_____

6. three

_____

_____

# Words with Long i

**Say and Write**

1. ride

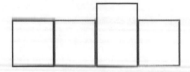

2. nine

3. five

4. hide

5. mine

6. time

The long i sound can be spelled i_e, like five and ride.

# Spell and Write

Write the spelling word that completes each sentence.

1. Where did the mouse _____?

2. I will share _____ with Mike.

3. What _____ is it?

4. The dog will _____ in the wagon.

5. There are _____ eggs left.

8 + 1 =

6. Eight and one make _____.

## Read and Write

Write the spelling words to complete the selection.

ride
nine
five
hide
mine
time

A bike contest can test how well you _____.

Don't run and _____.  Set up _____

big cones.  Ride around them one at a _____.

Ride slowly for four or _____ minutes.  Now you

are ready for the contest.  You might get to say, "The prize

is _____!"

# Proofreading

Circle each word that is spelled wrong.
Write the word correctly.

I like to ridee my bike.

I'm on it all the tim.

I got it when I was fiv.

1. _____

2. _____

3. _____

# Writing

Write two sentences about a bike.
Use two spelling words.

_____

_____

_____

_____

_____

## Word Puzzle

Write the spelling word for each clue.

game    made    take

**1.** It means "did make."

**2.** It means "to get."

**3.** People play this.

**1.** ↓

**2.** →

**3.** →

## Proofreading

Circle the word that is spelled wrong.
Write it correctly.

day    say    play

**4.** Clay wants to pla a game.

_____

**5.** What did you sae?

_____

**6.** What a great daay it is!

_____

# Dictionary Skills

Write the words in ABC order.

we    she    eat

_____

1. _____

2. _____

3. _____

# Missing Words

Write the word that completes each sentence.

keep    three    see

_____

4. I went to _____ a play.

5. One plus two is _____ .

6. May I _____ this puppy?

# More Words with Long i

**Say and Write**

1. my

2. by

3. fly

4. why

5. try

6. cry

The long i sound can be spelled y, like my and fly.

# Spell and Write

Write the spelling word that completes each sentence.

1. The baby began to _____,

2. That little bird wants to _____!

3. The cat knows _____ the vase fell.

4. I put on _____ coat.

5. She will _____ to skate.

6. The bag is _____ the door.

## Read and Write

Write the spelling words to complete the story.

my
by
fly
why
try
cry

_____

I made a kite.  I made _____ kite from a

_____

bag.  I wanted it to _____ up high.  People

_____          _____

stood _____ me.  They asked _____

_____

I used a bag.  I wanted to _____ it.  That's why.

_____

The bag did not fly very high, but I did not _____.

I just made another kite.

# Proofreading

Circle each word that is spelled wrong.
Write the word correctly.

This is miy bird.

He likes to flye.

He likes to sit bi me.

1. _____

2. _____

3. _____

# Writing

Write two sentences about a bird.
Use two spelling words.

_____

_____

_____

_____

_____

# Words with Long o

## Say and Write

1. so

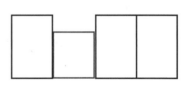

2. go

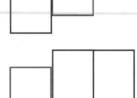

3. old

4. told

5. cold

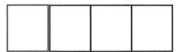

6. over

The long o sound can be spelled o, like go and cold.

## Spell and Write

Write the spelling word that completes each sentence.

1. The shop was closed, _____ we left.

2. Jo _____ Bo a joke.

3. Mom held the paper _____ her head.

4. The ball will _____ far.

5. The little dog was _____.

6. The big tree was very _____.

## Read and Write

Write the spelling words to complete the story.

so
go
old
told
cold
over

_____

JoJo wanted to _____ to a special place.

_____

She wanted to go _____ the rainbow.  JoJo

_____

packed an _____ bag.  She got her coat in case

_____          _____

it was _____.  JoJo _____ Gran

_____

about her plan.  Gran wanted to go, too, _____

they went together.  Good luck, JoJo and Gran!

# Proofreading

Circle each word that is spelled wrong.
Write the word correctly.

Mom,

May I ask Lin to come ovr?

She Is soo much fun.

Then can we goe for pizza?

Joey

1. _____

2. _____

3. _____

# Language Skills

Use was to write about one thing.
Use were to write about more than one thing.

Write the sentences. Use was and were correctly.

4. We _____ in an old store.

_____

5. Mom _____ by the milk.

_____

6. I told Mom I _____ cold.

_____

# More Words with Long o

## Say and Write

1. 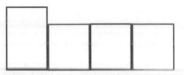 home

2. home

3. note

4. nose

5. road

6. coat

The long o sound can be spelled o_e or oa, like home and road.

## Spell and Write

Write the spelling word that completes each sentence.

1. I ride down the _____.

2. We _____ it rains today.

3. My _____ is green.

4. He has a big red _____.

5. Mr. Lo's _____ is in a big city.

6. Joan wrote me a _____.

## Read and Write

Write the spelling words to complete the story.

home
hope
note
nose
road
coat

One day Mole wanted to take a walk.  Dad was not at

_____  _____

_____.  Mole wrote Dad a _____.

_____

Then she walked down the _____.  She walked

_____

a long way.  A cold wind came.  Mole's _____

_____

was blue.  She wanted her warm _____.

_____

"I _____ I am not lost!" she said.  Then Mole

saw her house.  She smiled and went inside.

# Proofreading

Circle each word that is spelled wrong.
Write the word correctly.

Mom,

I lost my cote.

I hoap you arc not mad.

I will stay hoam to look for it.

Joan

1. _____

2. _____

3. _____

# Dictionary Skills

Circle the first letter of each word.
Then write the words in ABC order.

**4.** road    home    note

_____

_____

_____

**5.** told    nose    go

_____

_____

_____

# Words with the Vowel Sound in food

**Say and Write**

1. zoo

2. food

3. room

4. moon

5. soon

6. school

The vowel sound in food can be spelled oo, like zoo and school.

## Spell and Write

Write the spelling word that
completes each sentence.

1. What jumped over the _____?

2. Where do you go to _____?

3. Will cleaned his _____.

4. It will be dark _____.

5. We had fun at the _____.

6. Dad and Joel shop for _____.

## Read and Write

Write the spelling words to complete
the selection.

zoo
food
room
moon
soon
school

Would you like to camp at a _____? At one

zoo, you can sleep in a _____ with beds. You

can sleep under the _____ and stars, too. You

can give _____ to the animals. Your class from

_____ might want to go zoo camping. Find out

about zoo camping _____!

# Proofreading

Circle each word that is spelled wrong.
Write the word correctly.

I went on a schul trip.

We went to the zo.

We gave foode to the seals.

1. _____

2. _____

3. _____

# Writing

Write two sentences about a zoo.
Use two spelling words.

_____

_____

_____

_____

_____

_____

_____

# More Words with the Vowel Sound in food

**Say and Write**

1. too

2. who

3. two

4. do

5. shoe

6. you

> The vowel sound in food can be spelled oo, o, oe, or ou, like too, two, shoe, and you.

# Spell and Write

Write the spelling word that completes each sentence.

| too | do |
|-----|-----|
| who | shoe |
| two | you |

1. It's time to _____ our work.

2. The hat is _____ big.

3. Stu, where are _____?

4. Lou said, "I know _____ you are."

5. The bike has _____ wheels now.

6. Boo has my _____.

## Read and Write

Write the spelling words to complete
the selection.

too
who
two
do
shoe
you

_____

Look at your _____ feet.  Is there a

_____

_____ on each foot?  Shoes keep your feet safe.

_____

Shoes should not be _____ big or too small.

_____

No one knows _____ made the first

shoes.  Early people made them from animal skins.  Now

_____

_____ can buy shoes in a store.  What kind of

_____

shoes _____ you like to wear?

## Proofreading

Circle each word that is spelled wrong.
Write the word correctly.

Sue,

How much doo you like the circus?

I have tou tickets.

Will yoe come with me?

Dooley

1. _____

2. _____

3. _____

## Language Skills

Use to to mean into. Use too to mean more than enough.
Use two to mean the number after one.

Write the sentences. Use to, two, and too correctly.

4. Who are those _____ girls?

_____

5. That shoe is _____ big.

_____

6. Did they go _____ the store?

_____

## Missing Letter

Write y in each box. Then write the word.

my    why    try

**1.** tr ☐ = _____    **2.** wh ☐ = _____

**3.** m ☐ = _____

## Proofreading

Circle the word that is spelled wrong.
Write it correctly.

go    told    over

**4.** I can fly ovr a house.    _____

**5.** I can goa to the top of a tree.    _____

**6.** I toald my dad to look at me.    _____

# Rhyming Words

Help Toad find her way home. For each word on the trail, write the rhyming word from the box.

hope    road    coat

1. _____

2. _____

3. _____

# commonly misspelled words

| | | | |
|---|---|---|---|
| about | girl | one | too |
| am | have | or | two |
| and | her | our | very |
| are | him | outside | want |
| because | his | people | was |
| came | house | play | went |
| can | in | said | were |
| color | into | school | when |
| every | know | some | with |
| family | like | teacher | would |
| friend | little | their | your |
| friends | me | there | |
| get | my | they | |

| | | |
|---|---|---|
| the | to | very |
| and | all | your |
| a | for | good |
| you | said | take |
| of | they | how |
| he | so | about |
| it | in | know |
| I | with | any |
| had | there | their |
| we | can | here |
| was | them | after |
| at | like | before |
| she | would | old |
| but | come | been |
| on | long | who |
| | will | again |

# ANSWER KEY

**Page 8**
The letter **m** should be written for these problems: 1, 3, 4, 6, 7, 8, 9, 10, and 11.

**Page 9**
The letter **d** should be written for these problems: 1, 2, 4, 5, 6, 7, 9, 10, and 12.

**Page 10**
The letter **f** should be written for these problems: 1, 2, 4, 5, 6, 7, 10, 11, and 12.

**Page 11**
The letter **g** should be written for these problems: 1, 2, 3, 6, 7, 8, 9, 10, and 12.

**Page 12**
The letter **b** should be written for these problems: 1, 3, 4, 5, 6, 8, 9, 11, and 12.

**Page 13**
The letter **t** should be written for these problems: 1, 2, 4, 5, 7, 8, 9, 10, and 12.

**Page 14**
The letter **s** should be written for these problems: 1, 3, 4, 5, 6, 8, 10, 11, and 12.

**Page 15**
The letter **w** should be written for these problems: 1, 4, 5, 7, 10, and 11.

**Page 16**
The letter **k** should be written for these problems: 1, 2, 4, 5, 7, 8, 9, 10, and 11.

**Page 17**
The letter **j** should be written for these problems: 1, 3, 6, 8, 9, and 11.

**Page 18**
The letter **p** should be written for these problems: 1, 2, 4, 5, 7, 8, 10, 11, and 12.

**Page 19**
The letter **n** should be written for these problems: 1, 2, 3, 6, 7, 8, 9, 10, and 11.

**Page 20**
The letter **c** should be written for these problems: 1, 3, 4, 5, 6, 8, 10, 11, and 12.

**Page 21**
The letter **h** should be written for these problems: 1, 2, 4, 5, 7, 8, 9, 10, and 11.

**Page 22**
The letter **l** should be written for these problems: 1, 2, 3, 5, 6, 8, 9, 11, and 12.

**Page 23**
The letter **r** should be written for these problems: 1, 2, 4, 6, 7, 8, 9, 11, and 12.

**Page 24**
The letter **v** should be written for these problems: 1, 2, 4, 5, 6, and 11.

**Page 25**
The letter **y** should be written for these problems: 1, 3, 5, 7, 10, and 12.

**Page 26**
The letter **z** should be written for these problems: 1, 2, 5, 8, 9, and 11.

**Page 27**
The letters **qu** should be written for these problems: 1, 3, 5, 6. The letter **x** should be written for these problems: 8, 9, 10.

**Page 28**
1. m
2. f
3. b
4. k
5. s
6. d
7. m
8. g
9. j
10. t
11. d
12. w

**Page 29**
1. r
2. h
3. c
4. g
5. d
6. x
7. v
8. t
9. s
10. p
11. y
12. n
13. qu
14. z
15. w
16. m

**Page 30**
The letter **a** should be written for these problems: 1, 3, 4, 5, 7, 8, 9, 11, and 12.

**Page 31**
The letter **a** should be written for these problems and the pictures should be colored: 1, 2, 4, 6, 8, and 9.

**Page 32**

**Page 33**
1. fan
2. van
3. pan
4. man
5. can
6. tan
7. bat
8. cat
9. hat
10. mat
11. rat

**Page 34**
The letter **e** should be written for these problems: 1, 2, 4, 6, 7, 8, 9, 10, and 11.

**Page 35**
The letter **e** should be written for these problems and the pictures should be colored: 1, 2, 5, 6, 7, and 9.

**Page 36**

**Page 37**
1. bell
2. sell
3. shell
4. well
5. smell
6. hen
7. men
8. ten

**Page 38**
The letter **i** should be written for these problems: 1, 2, 3, 5, 7, 8, 10, 11, and 12.

**Page 39**
The letter **i** should be written for these problems and the pictures should be colored: 1, 3, 4, 5, 8, and 9.

**Page 40**

**Page 41**
1. hit
2. kit
3. sit
4. dig
5. pig
6. wig
7. big

**Page 42**
The letter **o** should be written for these problems: 1, 2, 3, 5, 6, 8, 9, 11, and 12.

**Page 43**
The letter **o** should be written for these problems and the pictures should be colored: 1, 2, 5, 6, 7, and 9.

**Page 44**

**Page 45**
1. hop
2. mop
3. pop
4. knot
5. dot
6. hot
7. pot

**Page 46**
The letter **u** should be written for these problems: 1, 2, 4, 6, 7, 8, 9, 11, and 12.

**Page 47**
The letter **u** should be written for these problems and the pictures should be colored: 1, 2, 4, 6, 7, and 9.

**Page 48**

**Page 49**
1. mug
2. hug
3. jug
4. bug
5. tug
6. rug
7. cut
8. hut
9. nut

**Page 50**
1. u; nut
2. i; bib
3. o; rod
4. e; web
5. a; map
6. e; vest
7. i; zip
8. u; duck
9. u; bug

**Page 51**
1. man
2. pop
3. pin
4. men
5. mop
6. fan
7. fin
8. pan
9. hen
10. nut
11. hop
12. cut

**Page 52**
For each problem, the word is written on the writing line and in the boxes.

**Page 53**
1. am
2. can
3. at
4. ran
5. fast
6. last

**Page 54**
Randy Rabbit **ran** on a path. The path was **at** the park. Randy ran well. He ran **fast**. That was **last** week. Now he will run again. "I **am** ready," Randy says. "I **can** do it!"

**Page 55**
1. at
2. can
3. am
4. Lad is fast.
5. We ran to Dad.
6. I was the last one.

**Page 56**
For each problem, the word is written on the writing line and in the boxes.

**Page 57**
1. van
2. that
3. hand
4. sat
5. have
6. has

**Page 58**
Nan **sat** with her dad. They sat in their **van**. Nan had a book in her **hand**. She got it from the library in her town. The library **has** many good books to read. Nan likes **that** library. Do you **have** a library where you live?

**Page 59**
1. van
2. has
3. that
4. We have a van.
5. I sat in back.
6. Mom held my hand.

**Page 60**
For each problem, the word is written on

142

the writing line and in the boxes.

**Page 61**
1. wet
2. red
3. ten
4. end
5. seven
6. tell

**Page 62**
Rex washes his socks. Some are red. Some are white. The socks are dripping wet. Rex puts them on the line. He has five pairs. There are ten socks on the line. Three socks on the end fall. Now only seven socks are on the line. Who will tell Rex?

**Page 63**
1. ten
2. seven
3. end
Answers to problems 4 to 7 will vary.

**Page 64**
For each problem, the word is written on the writing line and in the boxes.

**Page 65**
1. pet
2. when
3. best
4. went
5. get
6. help

**Page 66**
A puppy is a good pet. Would you like to get a puppy? You can help take care of it. You can feed your puppy when it is hungry. You can play with it. You will wonder where the time went. Do you think a puppy is the best pet?

**Page 67**
1. pet
2. when
3. best
Sentences written for the writing activity will vary. The sentence should include a spelling word.

**Page 68**
For each problem, the word is written on

**Page 69**
1. sick
2. with
3. is
4. in
5. quit
6. it

**Page 70**
Sometimes people get sick. Then they must stay in bed. It is not much fun. You can make a picture for a sick friend. Get some paper. Draw on it. Paint on it with bright colors. Don't quit until it looks great. Give it to your friend. Say, "Get well quick!"

**Page 71**
1. sick
2. is
3. in
4. it
5. quit
6. sick
7. with

**Page 72**
1. am
2. fast
3. can
4. have
5. has
6. that

**Page 73**
1. get
2. help
3. when
4. with
5. sick
6. in

**Page 74**
For each problem, the word is written on the writing line and in the boxes.

**Page 75**
1. six
2. if
3. sit
4. big
5. did
6. this

**Page 76**
I have six little kittens. My kittens will not always be little. Soon they will be big. The kittens sit on me. They go to sleep in

my lap. They wake up if I move. Then this is what they do. They cry, "Mew! Mew!" They did it just now!

**Page 77**
1. big
2. did
3. this
4. am; big; can
5. has; if; six
6. ran; sit; this

**Page 78**
For each problem, the word is written on the writing line and in the boxes.

**Page 79**
1. hop
2. stop
3. on
4. hot
5. not
6. top

**Page 80**
Bonnie likes to hop. She hops and hops. Bonnie hops on the path. She hops on the grass. She does not fall. Then she hops to the top of the hill. When will Bonnie stop? She will have to stop when she gets too hot!

**Page 81**
1. on
2. not
3. stop
4. Is Mopsy at the top?
5. Is Mopsy hot?
6. Will he hop down?

**Page 82**
For each problem, the word is written on the writing line and in the boxes.

**Page 83**
1. sock
2. mop
3. job
4. fox
5. lock
6. box

**Page 84**
Bob the ox had a job to do. He had to mop. A fox came in. He had a box. The fox took out a brush. "Put this on your sock," he said.

Bob did it. Then he put a brush on his other sock. He started to mop. "This is fast!" Bob said. "Soon I can lock up and go have fun!"

**Page 85**
1. job
2. box
3. mop
Sentences written for the writing activity will vary. The sentence should include a spelling word.

**Page 86**
For each problem, the word is written on the writing line and in the boxes.

**Page 87**
1. us
2. run
3. jump
4. duck
5. fun
6. much

**Page 88**
A baby duck is called a duckling. A duckling cannot run fast. A duckling can have fun. It can jump into the water. It can swim, too. The mother duck quacks if a duckling swims too far away. She is saying, "You have gone much too far. Come back to us!"

**Page 89**
1. us
2. fun
3. much
Sentences written for the writing activity will vary. The sentence should include a spelling word.

**Page 90**
For each problem, the word is written on the writing line and in the boxes.

**Page 91**
1. bus
2. must
3. cut
4. just
5. but
6. up

**Page 92**
Do you know what to do on a bus? You

must sit down when the bus is moving. You cannot stand up. You can play a game. You can sing a song, too. You can draw, but do not use scissors. You might cut yourself. You can read, or you can just sit and rest.

**Page 93**
1. just
2. bus
3. must
4. The cut is on my hand.
5. My house is up the street.
6. We are going home now.

**Page 94**
1. i; did
2. i; this
3. i; big
4. stop
5. on
6. not

**Page 95**

**Page 96**
For each problem, the word is written on the writing line and in the boxes.

**Page 97**
1. make
2. game
3. name
4. same
5. take
6. made

**Page 98**
What is your name? Play a game with your name. To begin, take the first letter of your name, such as P. Think of words that begin with the same letter. Next, make a sentence with the words. Then, add more words to the sentence you made.

**Page 99**
1. take
2. name
3. game
Sentences written for the writing activity will vary. The sentence should include a spelling word.

**Page 100**
For each problem, the word is written on the writing line and in the boxes.

**Page 101**
1. pay
2. day
3. stay
4. may
5. play
6. say

**Page 102**
Some work places have a special day. Children may go to work with an adult. They can stay all day. They learn about jobs. They have fun, but it is not a time to play. The children say they learn a lot. They see how adults work for their pay.

**Page 103**
1. stay
2. play
3. say
4. We may play with Jay all day.
5. He will pay Kay today.

**Page 104**
For each problem, the word is written on the writing line and in the boxes.

**Page 105**
1. we
2. eat
3. he
4. me
5. be
6. she

**Page 106**
My family sleeps a lot in winter. We need food before we sleep. We eat a lot! Today Mom showed me how to catch fish. Then she showed my brother. I know he likes fish. Soon we will find a cave. A cave is a good place to be in winter.

**Page 107**
1. be
2. we
3. he
4. My sister went with me.
5. She likes to be with me.
6. We went to eat pizza.

**Page 108**
For each problem, the word is written on the writing line and in the boxes.

**Page 109**
1. tree
2. street
3. feet
4. see
5. keep
6. three

**Page 110**
Dee's dad took her on a hike with **three** of her friends. They all live on the same **street**. "Please **keep** walking on the trail," Dad said. Something went splash! "What is on the other side of that **tree**?" Dad asked.
"I **see** a creek!" Lee said. "Some kids are in the water. May we get our **feet** wet, too?"

**Page 111**
1. tree
2. keep
3. feet
Answers to questions 4 to 6 will vary.

**Page 112**
For each problem, the word is written on the writing line and in the boxes.

**Page 113**
1. hide
2. mine
3. time
4. ride
5. five
6. nine

**Page 114**
A bike contest can test how well you **ride**. Don't run and **hide**. Set up **nine** big cones. Ride around them one at a **time**. Ride slowly for four or **five** minutes. Now you are ready for the contest. You might get to say, "The prize is **mine!**"

**Page 115**
1. ride
2. time
3. five
Sentences written for the writing activity will vary. Each sentence should include a spelling word.

**Page 116**
1. made
2. take
3. game
4. play
5. say
6. day

**Page 117**
1. eat
2. she
3. we
4. see
5. three
6. keep

**Page 118**
For each problem, the word is written on the writing line and in the boxes.

**Page 119**
1. cry
2. fly
3. why
4. my
5. try
6. by

**Page 120**
I made a kite. I made **my** kite from a bag. I wanted it to **fly** up high. People stood **by** me. They asked **why** I used a bag. I wanted to **try** it. That's why. The bag did not fly very high, but I did not **cry**. I just made another kite.

**Page 121**
1. my
2. fly
3. by
Sentences written for the writing activity will vary. Each sentence should include a spelling word.

**Page 122**
For each problem, the word is written on the writing line and in the boxes.

**Page 123**
1. so
2. told
3. over
4. go
5. cold
6. old

**Page 124**
JoJo wanted to **go** to a special place. She wanted to go **over** the rainbow. JoJo packed an **old** bag. She got her coat in case it was **cold**. JoJo **told** Gran about her plan. Gran wanted to go, too, **so** they went together. Good luck, JoJo and Gran!

**Page 125**
1. over
2. so
3. go
4. We were in an old store.
5. Mom was by the milk.
6. I told Mom I was cold.

**Page 126**
For each problem, the word is written on the writing line and in the boxes.

**Page 127**
1. road
2. hope
3. coat
4. nose
5. home
6. note

**Page 128**
One day Mole wanted to take a walk. Dad was not at **home**. Mole wrote Dad a **note**. Then she walked down the **road**. She walked a long way. A cold wind came. Mole's **nose** was blue. She wanted her warm **coat**. "I **hope** I am not lost!" she said. Then Mole saw her house. She smiled and went inside.

**Page 129**
1. coat
2. hope
3. home

**Page 130**
For each problem, the word is written on the writing line and in the boxes.

**Page 131**
1. moon
2. school
3. room
4. soon
5. zoo
6. food

**Page 132**
Would you like to camp at a **zoo**? At one zoo, you can **sleep** in a **room** with beds. You can sleep under the **moon** and stars, too. You can give **food** to the animals. Your class from **school** might want to go zoo camping. Find out about zoo camping **soon!**

**Page 133**
1. school
2. zoo
3. food
Sentences written for the writing activity will vary. Each sentence should include a spelling word.

**Page 134**
For each problem, the word is written on the writing line and in the boxes.

**Page 135**
1. do
2. too
3. you
4. who
5. two
6. shoe

**Page 136**
Look at your **two** feet. Is there a **shoe** on each foot? Shoes keep your feet safe. Shoes should not be **too** big or too small.
No one knows **who** made the first shoes. Early people made them from animal skins. Now **you** can buy shoes in a store. What kind of shoes **do** you like to wear?

**Page 137**
1. do
2. two
3. you
4. Who are those two girls?
5. That shoe is too big.
6. Did they go to the store?

**Page 138**
1. try
2. why
3. my
4. river
5. go
6. told

**Page 139**
1. coat
2. hope
3. road